Why Are the Rain Forests Being Destroyed?

Why Are the Rain Forests Being Destroyed?

Peter Littlewood

ARCTURUS

This edition first published in 2010 by Arcturus Publishing
Distributed by Black Rabbit Books
P.O. Box 3263
Mankato
Minnesota MN 56002

Printed in the United States

Series concept: Alex Woolf
Editors: Jonathan Hilton and Karen Taschek
Designer: Ian Winton
Picture researcher: Jonathan Hilton

Library of Congress Cataloging-in-Publication Data

Littlewood, Peter.
  Why are the rainforests being destroyed? / by Peter Littlewood.
     p. cm. -- (Global questions)
  Includes bibliographical references and index.
  Summary: "This series takes an in-depth look at some of the major issues and crises that are on the front pages of today's newspapers. Each book looks at the historical background to the questions and offers balanced reporting of the situation and several solutions to the problem. Features include timelines, maps and primary sources"--Provided by publisher.
  ISBN 978-1-84837-688-5 (library binding : alk. paper)
  1. Rain forest ecology--Juvenile literature. 2. Rain forests--Juvenile literature. I. Title.
  QH541.5.R27L49 2011
  333.75--dc22

                    2010011024

Picture credits:
Corbis: 6 (Collart Herve/Sygma), 8 (George Steinmetz), 9 (Fernando Bizerra Jr/epa), 10 (Louise Murray/Robert Harding World Imagery), 12 (Gerd Ludwig), 13 (Carlos Cazalis), 14 (Kazuyoshi Nomachi), 15 (Wayne Lawler; Ecoscene), 16–17 (Collart Herve/Sygma), 19 (Gustavo Gilabert/Saba), 20 (Douglas Engle), 22 (Frans Lanting), 25 (Daisy Gilardini/Science Faction), 26 (Staffan Widstrand), 27 (Colin McPherson), 28 (Bettmann), 29 (Paolo Aguilar), 31 (David Muench), 32 (David Mercado/Reuters), 33 (Jason Hawkes), 35 (Tom Brakefield), 36 (Jeremy Horner), 37 (Andy Aitchison), 38 (Ludo Kuipers), 39 (Bob Krist), 40 (Fernando Bengoechea/Beateworks), 41 (Barry Lewis/In Pictures), 42 (Janet Jarman).
Press Association Images: 34 (John Stillwell/PA Wire).
Science Photo Library: cover (Jacques Jangoux), 11 (David Nicholls), 24 (Gary Hincks).
Shutterstock: title page (Jose AS Reyes), 23 (All32), 30 (Eric Gevaert), 43 (E Sweet).

Cover caption: A rain forest being burned to clear land for cattle. Rain forest is also cleared to make way for crops, including soybeans, coffee, and palm oil, or for mining or oil drilling.
Title page caption: Once mighty rain forest trees are cut down and chopped into logs ready for export.

SL001358US   Supplier 02 Date 0510

Contents

Chapter 1

Why do we need the rain forests?

Picture yourself deep in a forest. Looking up, you can just see the sunlight glinting through the dense canopy of leaves high above your head. Your clothes are soaked in sweat and the heat is almost stifling. All around, you can hear the buzz of insects, the hoots of monkeys, and the calls of colorful birds darting about high in the canopy. An occasional grunt or growl from ground level gives you some cause for concern. Then, suddenly, lightning flashes overhead. You jump at the sound of thunder and

Lush, green, and seemingly endless, in reality the planet's dense tropical rain forests are under considerable threat. Rain forests may once have covered up to 12 percent of the world's land surface. Now they cover only about half that area.

almost immediately are drenched by a heavy downpour of rain. You are in a rain forest, one of the most fascinating and diverse habitats anywhere on the planet.

Rain forests today

Tropical rain forests are dense, evergreen forests that receive over 8.2 feet (2.5 meters) of rain each year. They are found across the world between the Tropics of Cancer and Capricorn (23.5 degrees north and south of the equator). They occur in Asia, Africa, South America, northern Australia, and on many tropical islands. They cover about 6 percent of the planet's land surface—about 5.9 million square miles (15 million square kilometers). The largest rain forest, the Amazon in South America, spans eight different countries and covers an area of almost 2 million square miles (5.2 million square kilometers).

Rain forest climate

It rains a lot in a rain forest—mostly in the afternoons. Although rainforests experience annual rainfall of at least 98.4 inches (2.5 meters), some receive up to 400 inches (10 meters) of rain each year—that's about 10 times the annual average for New York City. Temperatures rarely fall below 68°F (20°C) and can exceed 86°F (30°C), giving annual average temperatures of about 77°F (25°C). Humidity in the rain forest can reach up to 100 percent—saturation point. And since the sun is almost directly overhead throughout the year, there are no distinct seasons.

Rain forest inhabitants

The plants of the rain forest are well adapted to their environment. Trees grow up to 230 feet (60 meters tall)—the tallest recorded grew to 272 feet (83 meters). Their leaves are concentrated high up in the canopy. Many have huge buttress roots to help anchor them to the ground and soak up nutrients from the soil. Below them are other plants adapted to living in the shrub and floor layers. A huge range of animals, such as jaguars, anacondas, piranhas, orangutans, and parrots, can be found in the world's rain forests. Living among them are tribes of native people, such as the Kayapo and Yanomami, who have lived in harmony with their forest environment for thousands of years.

Expert View

Naturalist Charles Darwin recorded these impressions of the forests outside of Rio de Janeiro:

"The forest abounded with beautiful objects . . . It is not possible to give an adequate idea of the higher feelings of wonder, astonishment and devotion, which fill and elevate the mind."

Charles Darwin, **The Voyage of the Beagle,** *1832*

A fragile paradise

Rain forests hold incredibly rich stores of animal and plant life. A third of the world's plant life grows in the rain forests, and each 1.2 square yards (one square meter) can support up to 177 pounds (80 kilograms) of living material (biomass).

It is known that more than half of the world's animal and plant species live in the rain forests, and a single acre can contain 80 different tree species and more than 16,200 species of insect. In just 25 acres (10 hectares) of Malaysian rain forest,

This selection of butterflies comes from one small area of rain forest in the Central African Republic. Each species lives on its own specific tree and emerges once a year to coincide with a key event in the tree's life cycle, such as flowering.

780 different species of tree were discovered. That is more than the total number of tree species that are native to all of the US and Canada.

Amazingly, given the vast number of species rain forests support, their soils are shallow and acidic. In fact, their soils are among the poorest in the world, and heavy rainfall washes away any nutrients that are not taken up by the trees. Rain forests are able to thrive because they feed on themselves—dead plant and animal matter decays quickly on the forest floor and the shallow-rooted trees quickly absorb the nutrients released.

Treading lightly

People have lived in harmony with the rain forest for thousands of years, with a way of life that went almost unchanged for centuries. In the Amazon, tribes such as the Yanomami, Kayapo, and Yekuana have learned to conserve the resources of their forest home. They know never to take too much from the forest. They hunt for meat, grow crops, and gather fruits and nuts. They use many of the plants and animals to provide medicines for their people and poisons for hunting.

Unfortunately, the tribes' encounters with "civilization" have often led to disaster for them. It is estimated that the Amazon rain forest supported about 6 million tribal people before 1500 CE. By the year 2000, there were fewer than 250,000 left. More than 90 tribes are thought to have disappeared just from the Amazon during the twentieth century alone. Many were wiped out when Western settlers brought diseases they had never encountered before—such as measles—which alone killed thousands of tribespeople.

Expert View

Anthropologist Flora Lu Holt lived with the Huaorani in the Amazonian rain forest for more than 10 years:

"I think that the Huaorani are capable of making good decisions. I think that they can adopt certain things from Western culture or choose not to. What's important is that they have that choice."

Flora Lu Holt

Now some of the tribes, such as the Yanomami, have protected homelands in government-approved reservations, and they are more able to maintain their traditions. The way of life of the forest peoples is as fragile as the forests they live in. They could teach us much, but most prefer to be left alone to continue living as they always have, in harmony with their surroundings.

The Waura people from the Brazilian Amazon were almost wiped out by disease in the 1950s after they came into contact with the industrialized world. They have now been vaccinated against diseases such as tetanus, influenza, and measles, and as a result, the tribe now numbers around 400 individuals again.

Rain forest products

A large number of everyday foodstuffs that we enjoy today have their origins in the rain forests of the world. For example, bananas, peppers, peanuts, coffee, tea, cola, cocoa, vanilla, sugar, and many spices all come from the world's rain forests, although some have been adapted over the years to grow in other climate zones. Valuable tropical woods, including mahogany, teak, rosewood, and sandalwood, are used to make furniture, ornaments, and perfumes.

In the home, oils, gums, and resins that have been sourced from the rain forests are found in such everyday items as soaps, varnish, and wood-finishing products; fuel; paint; insecticides; detergents; and disinfectants.

Rain forest medicines

Perhaps even more important than the household products we are all familiar with are the medicines that originate in the rain forest. So far, more than 2,000 rain forest plants have been identified as having anti-cancer properties. Scientists have tested only 10 percent of these plants and have studied only 1 percent of them in detail. About 25 percent of all medicines used by people in the US are made from ingredients originating in the rain forest.

Curare, which is a substance extracted from a rain forest vine, is commonly used in carefully measured doses in surgery as a muscle relaxant. However, tribal peoples use curare in stronger doses as a poison on darts and arrows when hunting. The rosy periwinkle from the rain forests of Madagascar, off the east coast of Africa, is used to treat leukemia. Who knows how many other cures remain undiscovered deep in the forests?

Climate regulation

Rain forests store a colossal amount of water—it is thought that up to half of the world's rainwater

Moisture that evaporates from the forest gathers in clouds above the canopy. When the vapor condenses, it creates the conditions for the forest's daily downpour.

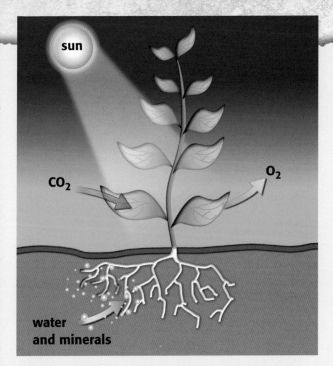

Photosynthesis in action. Water absorbed by the plant's roots combines with carbon dioxide (CO_2) from the air and sunlight to produce starch (energy for the plant) and oxygen (O_2).

is stored in rain forests. The trees draw in the water and release it into the atmosphere through evaporation as swirling mists and clouds. The rain forests recycle huge amounts of water every day, and this helps to feed rivers, lakes, and irrigation systems, preventing droughts and the famine and disease that follow them.

The lungs of the planet

During the day rain forests absorb carbon dioxide (CO_2) from the atmosphere. The plants make their food using a process called photosynthesis. In photosynthesis, leaves absorb carbon dioxide from the air, combine it with water sucked up by the plant's roots, and, with the aid of sunlight, convert them into sugars. This provides the fuel the plants need to survive. As a by-product of photosynthesis, plants produce oxygen (O_2), which is released into the atmosphere. The vast number of trees and other plants growing in the rain forests help to maintain the balance of carbon dioxide and oxygen in the atmosphere throughout the entire world.

With their enormous range of animal and plant species, the foods, materials, and medicines they provide, and the crucial contribution they make to circulating the planet's water and regulating the world's atmosphere, the rain forests are enormously important. Yet despite all of this, they are being destroyed at an alarming rate.

FORUM

When you see pictures of the rain forests, there are so many trees it seems impossible that they could all be destroyed. It requires a little imagination to realize they are all under threat:

"The rain forests are miles away—why should I care?"

Student, US

"They may be far away, but the world needs the rain forests and you probably use products from the rain forest every day."

Teacher, US

What's your opinion?

Chapter 2

What are the threats to the rain forest?

It is amazing how a simple act such as building a road can cause so much damage in the rain forest. Where roads have been created to open up areas that were previously inaccessible, tens of thousands of settlers and developers have followed. As an initial consequence, the newcomers push out the native peoples, who may have been living undisturbed in the forest for centuries.

Roads across the rain forest

The Trans-Amazonian Highway, built in the 1970s, stretches 2,000 miles (3,200 kilometers) across the Amazon from east to west in northern Brazil. The Brazilian government's plan was to create settlements in previously unused areas. They offered settlers 250-acre (100-hectare) plots, six months' salary, and easy access to agricultural loans. Costs spiraled and the project ended up costing $65,000 per family settled. Because the forest soils were so unstable and easily eroded, the road was often impassable, harvests failed, and in some places, up to 46 tons (50 metric tons) of soil per acre of land were washed away into the rivers during the rains.

The destructive effects of road building in the rain forests can be clearly seen in this photograph. While the forest on the right remains untouched, that to the left is a scene of utter devastation.

This soybean plantation located in Brazil stretches over some 1.2 million acres (494,000 hectares) and produces more than 660,000 tons (600,000 metric tons) of soybeans per year. Virgin rain forest is cut down and destroyed to make way for soybean plantations.

More recently, plans have been drawn up to improve another road through the Brazilian Amazon, BR-163, which stretches for 1,100 miles (1,770 kilometers) from Cuiaba, near the Bolivian border, to Santarem, on the banks of the Amazon. About 600 miles (965 kilometers) of it is still dirt track, but the Brazilian government plans to pave all of it—and this is a real cause for concern among environmentalists.

Agriculture

The first 450 miles (725 kilometers) of BR-163 is already paved. On either side of it, for as far as the eye can see, what was once forest is now rolling fields. The main crop grown is soybeans, half of which is exported to countries in the European Union. The soya crop is the main reason for paving the rest of BR-163. Santarem has a deep-water port, and a paved BR-163 would shorten the journey of the soybean crop by 600 miles (965 kilometers) over land and by a similar distance by sea, saving on transportation costs and increasing producers' profits.

The forests surrounding the unpaved section of BR-163 are much less affected by human activities, but they are also lawless, with murders frequently committed. Most murders involve disputes about land—although the government encouraged many people to settle in the region, only a few were given legal title to land. Now the most violent have the most land.

FOCUS

"You used to see tapirs, capybaras, even jaguars by the side of the road. Now you hardly see anything. When the paving comes, you'll be able to get everything out—and you will finish off the forest completely."

Gustavo Hering, truck driver on BR-163

Logging

Rain forests are full of valuable trees. For many years, people have harvested the high-value hardwoods found growing there, such as teak and mahogany, to supply the timber markets of Europe, Japan, and the US. The damage this does to the forests has now been recognized, so many logging companies are trying to reduce the impact of their activities by taking only 'selected' trees and allowing the forest to regrow naturally.

The problem is that only a certain amount of damage reduction that can be done. The big, valuable trees do not tend to live close to each other, meaning that logging operations spread out over a wide area of rain forest. When a large tree is felled, it brings down many smaller trees around it, along with the vines, such as lianas (a tropical plant), and other climbers growing on it.

The damage caused to the surrounding forest when huge trees are felled, such as this one in the rain forests of Borneo, is considerable.

Removing the trees once they have been cut down causes further destruction: the massive logging vehicles used in the process need to gain access to the felled trees, which often means plowing through areas of forest and destroying all the smaller trees in the way. It is estimated that in Southeast Asia, up to 75 percent of the trees remaining after logging have been either damaged or killed.

In addition to the physical damage done to the trees, the tracks left by the vehicles leave the soil exposed. The rains then wash the soil into the rivers, which causes a buildup of silt and eventual flooding.

More roads mean more people

Loggers build roads through the forest so that they can easily access the logging sites, which are generally established in formerly untouched forest. When the loggers have left, the roads remain, providing landless farmers with a means of getting into what was previously inaccessible territory, creating yet more destruction. In all, an estimated 12 million acres (5 million hectares) of rain forest are lost to logging each year.

A sustainable future?

Modern "sustainable" hardwood plantations are becoming more common. However, since it takes more than 60 years for most hardwood trees to grow to a size large enough to be felled, the timelines involved in these sustainable projects are long and it is questionable just how sustainable they will ultimately prove to be.

Each time trees are felled, habitats for the birds, mammals, and other wildlife that lived there are lost. Because regrowth takes so long, once a habitat has been destroyed, the creatures that lived there have to move on or die. It simply takes too long for the forest to grow back.

Here a road in Kalimantan, Borneo, built by commercial loggers has given settlers access to land that was previously unreachable. The damage caused by the settlements they create means that the forest can never recover.

Mining the forests

Many rain forest areas are rich in such minerals as copper, bauxite (aluminium ore), iron ore, gold, and diamonds. Mining is an environmentally damaging process and in the rain forest the destructive effects of this activity are more pronounced. And in order to reach the mining areas, yet more roads are built through the forests.

Massive environmental pollution has been caused by the mining operations themselves. For example, during a gold rush in Brazil that began in 1980, at least 250,000 people moved to Serra Pelada in Pala State, where the gold had been discovered. Mercury, a highly toxic metal, was used to separate the gold from the soil around it, and an estimated 9,900 tons (9,000 metric tons) of mercury ended up in the region's rivers, along with huge amounts of sediment. The sewage produced by the miners, along with other litter, also ended up in the rivers.

This image from Carajas, Brazil, shows just a small part of the world's largest iron mine. Environmental damage results from the clearance of the forest and the use of toxic chemicals in the mining process, which end up in nearby rivers.

Harnessing the power of water

With more people moving into rain forest regions, there is an ever-increasing demand for energy. The mighty rivers of the Amazon rain forest have huge potential for creating electricity by moving water at high speeds through turbines, which are like giant propellers. The technical term for creating electricity with water is hydroelectric power, or HEP.

The amount of irreversible environmental damage caused by HEP schemes is huge. Dams are built in rain forest valleys, often in places where native tribes have lived for hundreds, if not thousands of years. Once a dam is in place, the valley slowly floods, destroying the rain forest and the habitat of countless millions of animals—from primates to insects—forever, as well as forcing any people living in the path of the floodwaters to move out of the way.

Although the impact of hydroelectric power on the rain forest is enormous, at least the result of the destruction is clean, carbon-free energy. Arguably, countries such as Brazil need to harness HEP—here being produced by the Tucurui Dam in Brazil—in order to continue their development.

The biggest project in the Amazon is the Tocantins River Basin Hydroelectric Project, which will convert the Tocantins River into a string of lakes and 27 hydroelectric dams stretching for nearly 1,240 miles (2,000 kilometers). By 2006, five dams had been constructed on the Tocantins. The first, at Tucurui, flooded 1,115 square miles (2,860 square kilometers) of forest and forced more than 40,000 people to leave home.

FORUM

The debate between those wanting to exploit the forests for short-term benefits and those who want to protect the long-term health of the environment is often passionate. Although passionate, the arguments are not always clear cut:

"There are so many resources in the forest that could help my country to develop. We have to make use of them."

Government minister, Indonesia

"We shouldn't destroy any more forest. It's just too important for the health of the planet."

Environmental campaigner

What's your opinion?

The search for oil

Some of the planet's most promising oil and gas deposits are deep in the world's rain forest. In the past, some oil companies have paid little attention to the damage they caused in the rain forest. For example, in the Oriente region of Ecuador, US oil company Texaco spilled an estimated 20 million gallons (77 million liters) of crude oil and dumped 33 million gallons (127 million liters) of toxic chemicals into rivers during 28 years of oil drilling.

Chapter 3

How is agriculture a threat?

In the past, indigenous (native) people used to clear small areas of rain forest in order to create gardens where they could grow enough crops to survive. They added to their stores of food by gathering fruit and nuts that grew naturally and by hunting. They moved on to a fresh patch of forest every few years, and their abandoned gardens soon became overgrown as the rain forest repaired itself.

From forest to farm

In modern times, this low-impact form of land use has changed as huge areas of rain forest have been cleared for plantations, where a single "cash crop"—a crop such as sugar, soybeans, or coffee, which provides maximum profit—can be planted. The plantations are often controlled by internationally owned companies based overseas.

Cash crops are grown to make money quickly, showing little concern for the environmental damage caused. The thin rain forest soils are farmed intensively using fertilizers, pesticides, and modern machinery that tears at the structure of the land itself. After only a few years, the delicate soil has lost most of its nutrients, which means that less of the crops can be grown. When crop yields, and therefore profits, become too low, the farmers often simply abandon the land. They move on to open up and destroy more areas of rain forest, setting up new farms as they go.

In the past, the effects of intensive agriculture on rain forest soils were unknown, but now it is well established that the soils cannot support intensive agriculture for long before they become barren.

FOCUS

"We did not destroy this region. We transformed this region from native vegetation to agricultural production. What you are seeing here is how we are supporting humanity. You cannot survive without eating food."

Nelson Piccoli, farmer, Sorriso, Brazil

Burning has long been used as a means of clearing areas of rain forest to make way for agriculture. Although individual farmers burn only small areas each year, the combined effect of hundreds of thousands of these farms is huge.

Despite this, the pace of intensive agriculture has increased. It is driven by the short-term interest of the controlling companies and the need for local farmers to earn money to support their families in the poorer countries where the rain forests are found.

Shifting cultivation

Huge numbers of indigenous people are forced off their land by governments or business corporations to make way for the plantations. Many follow roads into areas of rain forest that are already damaged by logging, mining, and oil exploration. Often they are encouraged to move into former logging sites by their national governments. A popular slogan in Brazil recently was "Land without men for men without land."

Using a technique called "slash and burn," small-scale farmers clear an area of forest by cutting down the big trees and setting fire to the rest. They grow their few crops in the forest but after a time run they into the same problems as the cash-crop growers. The soil does not remain fertile for long, so they are forced to move on. Shifting cultivation is thought to be responsible for up to 60 percent of tropical forest loss. In the Brazilian Amazon alone, about 500,000 small-scale farmers are responsible for clearing an estimated 2.5 acres (one hectare) each per year.

Clearing rain forest for cows

Vast areas of the Amazon rain forest are cleared each year to make way for huge cattle herds. In fact, cattle ranching is now the biggest cause of deforestation in the Amazon. In the last 20 years, Costa Rica has lost the majority of its forests to this activity.

Brazil has the largest cattle herds in the world—more than 200 million animals—which means that there are more cows in Brazil than there are people. It has been the biggest exporter of beef on the planet since 2003, and almost 80 percent of the deforested Brazilian Amazon is now used for cattle ranching.

Despite this, the Brazilian government has a stated objective of doubling its share of the world beef market to 60 percent by 2018. In a contradictory move, it also aims to reduce

Huge areas of rain forest have already been cleared to provide grazing for Brazil's immense and growing cattle herds. There are already more than 200 million cattle in Brazil—more than one cow for every member of the human population.

Expert View

Signs indicate the difficulty of increasing beef production while decreasing the output of greenhouse gases:

"The Brazilian government needs to get a grip on the cattle industry before it completely undermines the country's chances of tackling climate change. Right now, huge swathes of rain forest are being cut down to feed the global appetite for beef and leather."

Sarah Sharoka, Greenpeace Forests Campaigner

deforestation by 72 percent by 2017 as part of a national action plan to combat climate change. Achieving both targets at once will be almost impossible.

Greenhouse gases

Brazil is already the fourth-biggest emitter of greenhouse gases after Indonesia (another major rain forest country), the US, and China. Three-quarters of its carbon dioxide (CO_2) emissions are the result of the burning of rain forest, with much of the rest being caused by the cattle industry through "bovine methane emissions" (cow farts). You'd have gas too if all you ate every day was grass.

An area of rain forest the size of Portugal, which measures approximately 25 million acres (10 million hectares), was cleared between 1996 and 2006 in the Mato Grosso region of Brazil alone to make way for the huge cattle herds, mostly by setting fire to virgin forest. About 40 percent of the national herd is now living on land that used to be rain forest. If the expansion of Brazil's beef herd continues through the destruction of yet more rain forest, then the country stands little chance of meeting its targets for the reduction of greenhouse gas emissions.

Diminishing returns

As we now know, rain forest soils are very poor and lose their fertility fairly quickly once the forest cover is removed. At first, each acre will support a couple of cows, but within eight years, those cows will need five times as much land to find enough food to survive. To overcome this, the ranchers simply move on, destroying yet more of the forest in the process. As a rough guide, for every pound of beef produced for the world markets about 20 square yards (16.5 square meters) of rain forest are destroyed.

Growing fuel from forest

Palm oil plantations are the biggest cause of rain forest loss in Malaysia and Indonesia. In what is becoming a familiar pattern, rain forest is cleared away so that palm trees can be planted. This destroys all the rain forest plant species that lived there and forces any animals dependent on the native plants to either move deeper into the forest or die.

Palm oil plantations have expanded extremely rapidly in Indonesia—the area of land occupied by plantations has doubled in the last 10 years, threatening endangered species such as the orangutan and Sumatran tiger with extinction. The burning of its rain forests to clear ground for the establishment of palm oil plantations is the reason that Indonesia is now the world's third-largest emitter of CO_2.

What do we do with palm oil?

Palm oil is a vegetable oil and is an inexpensive ingredient found in a range of products from chocolate to detergents. It is found in about one in 10 food products in the supermarket.

Cars and palm oil

Palm oil is added as "biofuel" to the diesel sold to most motorists in the United Kingdom. In 2008, British motorists used 7 million gallons (27 million liters) of palm oil from Indonesia and 17 million gallons (64 million liters) from Malaysia. Other countries supplied another 19 million gallons (32 million liters). Almost all of this palm oil came from land that was previously occupied by rain forest.

This area of rain forest has been cleared to plant oil palms. World demand for palm oil continues to grow, and it is increasingly being used as a biofuel to comply with laws that have been drafted to protect the environment.

With increasing pressure on oil companies to produce more biofuel, ever larger areas of rain forest are being destroyed each year to make way for palm oil plantations. It is clear that biofuel is not going to solve our environmental problems.

In theory at least, palm oil is less environmentally damaging than non-renewable fossil fuels, such as oil, because crops absorb CO_2 (which is the most important greenhouse gas) as they grow. But to make way for the palm plantations, the rain forests are cleared by burning This releases huge quantities of CO_2 into the atmosphere. It has been estimated that it would take a palm oil plantation up to 840 years to soak up the carbon that was released by burning the forest to make way for that same plantation.

A European Union initiative, ironically one that is trying to reduce greenhouse gas emissions, states that 3.25 percent of all fuel currently sold by oil companies has to be biofuel. By 2020, oil companies are expected to be selling 13 percent biofuel as a percentage of their total fuel sales. Most diesel now has about 5 percent palm oil.

FORUM

Points of view regarding the fate of the rain forest could not be more different:

"The forest is very important to us because it gives fruit, rivers from where we drink, we eat fish from there too. In the forest, the air is clean and nature nurtures people. It's life, it preserves our life."

Davi Kopenawa, Yanomami tribe

"Not to exploit and populate this region [Amazonia] is a luxury Brazil cannot afford. What is more important, man or a tree?"

Former Commander of the Amazon Region

What's your opinion?

Chapter 4

What happens when the rain forests are destroyed?

Climate change is always in the news, but we don't often hear about the key role that rain forests have in regulating the planet's climate. Rain forests absorb carbon dioxide and release oxygen through the process of photosynthesis (see page 11). Although they emit CO_2 at night, they emit less than they absorb, which means that they help to reduce overall levels of CO_2 in the atmosphere. Even more importantly, rain forests act as stores of carbon. The carbon contained within the trees is released as CO_2 when they are burned or even when they are simply left to decay. It is estimated that the remaining forests contain 1.1 trillion tons (one trillion metric tons) of CO_2.

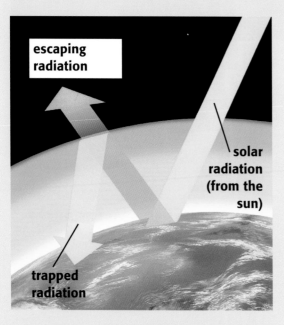

escaping radiation

solar radiation (from the sun)

trapped radiation

When solar radiation passes through our atmosphere, some is absorbed while some is reflected away back into space. But as greenhouse gases build up, less radiation excapes back into space and more is trapped, raising the planet's temperature.

An unequal balance

It could be (and has been) argued that by planting crops where once there was rain forest, the crops are still absorbing CO_2 and releasing oxygen, just as the forest did. However, an area of crops will absorb about a hundred times less CO_2 than the same area of rain forest—and the amounts of rain forest that are involved are enormous. It is estimated that 49,980,450 acres (20,235,000 hectares)—an area of land that is larger than Minnesota—is being destroyed each year.

Burning issues

Deforestation accounts for up to 25 percent of human greenhouse gas emissions worldwide each year—or 4.2 billion tons (2 billion metric tons) per year. To give you an idea of just how huge that is, the planet's transportation and industry account for only about 14 percent each. Air travel, often cited as the biggest evil in climate change, accounts for only 3 percent of total greenhouse gas emissions. In the next four years, burning rain forests is likely to pump out more CO_2 than every flight that has ever taken place or will take place until 2025. So, if we can save the rain forests, we stand a much better chance of fighting climate change.

Rain, rain, go away

Rain forests help to control rainfall across the planet. They draw up huge amounts of water from the soil, and most of this evaporates into the atmosphere, where the water vapor collects in clouds and rains back down onto the forest. Whereas evaporation from the oceans provides most of the planet's rainwater, inland areas on huge continents such as South America are kept from turning into desert by the rain forests, which recycle rainfall across the land. As forests are cut down, the water-recycling service grows weaker, and inland areas become gradually drier.

The evaporation of water from the leaves and soil takes energy from the land and keeps it cooler—just as we feel cooler when the sweat on our skin evaporates. Evaporation of water from land forms clouds, which help to reflect the sun's heat into space. So when we destroy rain forest, we not only release CO_2 into the atmosphere, but we warm the planet more through reduced evaporation leading to reduced cloud formation.

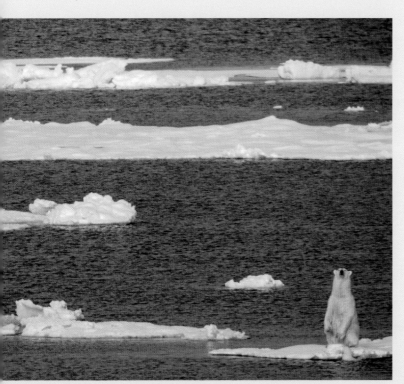

The effects of climate change as a result of rain forest destruction are being felt across the globe. Here polar bears in the Russian Arctic are stranded on a small ice floe in an area that was once solid sea ice.

First come the floods

Burning or cutting down rain forest doesn't stop rainwater recycling immediately. Once an area has been cleared of the trees that protected the fragile forest soil, it loses its ability to absorb the huge amounts of rainwater that fall on it. The soil is easily washed away, ending up in the rivers as silt. Fish and many aquatic plants depend on clean water to live in, so as the rivers silt up, the fish and plants start to disappear.

Soil has been washed into this river from areas of cleared rain forest. Although this is not an immediate threat to canopy dwellers, ground-based species flee or drown, and fish and aquatic plants struggle in the silty waters.

In many cases, heavy rains falling on deforested areas roll right off the soil, and can cause flooding or mud slides. In El Salvador, where all but 2 percent of the original tree cover has now been removed, flash floods and mud slides have become commonplace. As an example, in October 2005, the small town of Colon was affected by mud slides and flooding as a result of heavy rain caused by tropical storm Stan, resulting in the deaths of at least 39 people.

Meanwhile, in China, about 30 percent of its tropical forests were cut down in the 1980s and 1990s. Where the trees were cleared, soil

FOCUS

The end of a way of life

"There will be floods if the trees go, and where will we hunt and get our building materials? Perhaps we will see the end of the life we know."

Pius Ongyang, a 67-year-old leader of the Tumugung tribe, Malaysia

was easily eroded from the mountainous areas and washed downstream, settling as silt and building up on the riverbed, raising the level of the river water. When heavy rains came, the rivers couldn't cope and burst their banks. In 1999, this contributed to huge flooding on the Yellow and Yangtze rivers and the deaths of more than 4,000 people.

Then come the deserts

Over time, the rains will stop falling over some areas where the rain forest has been cleared. These areas are often well away from the coast in places where rainwater recycling by the forests was responsible for keeping the area well watered. The rains often stop only after much of the soil has been washed away. The increased heat—caused by a lack of water vapor in the air and the lack of shade that used to be provided by the trees coupled with a lack of fresh rainfall—can turn areas into dry, lifeless deserts.

What soil is left is soon lacking in nutrients because the minerals are washed away and there is no dead plant and animal matter decaying into the soil to enrich it. This process is called desertification. Once the nutrient cycle is broken, it is almost impossible to fix. To repair the forest, you would have to enrich the soil with fertilizers, plant fairly mature trees so that the soil was protected from rainfall, and care for the replanted area for many years to ensure adequate tree regrowth.

A few scattered trees are all that are left after an area of rain forest has been cleared. Without the forest to regulate rainfall, the land is already in the process of drying out. In a few years, almost nothing will be able to grow here.

When cultures collide

When areas of rain forest are destroyed, it's not just the trees that disappear. When new industries move into areas of forest that were previously untouched by "civilization," they often come across tribes who have lived in harmony with the forests for centuries.

The collision of cultures is rarely a happy one. In centuries past, tribal people were captured to be sold as slaves or were hunted down. Many died from diseases brought in by the new settlers to their lands that they had never encountered before—some of which modern Western medicine can easily cure. These included measles, tuberculosis, malaria, and worms. Even the common cold can be fatal to people who have no natural immunity to it.

Hiding from the world

Almost unbelievably, there are still tribes deep in the forests that have never made contact with the modern world. This is not difficult to understand when you consider

the fate of the Akunsu tribe, from the Rondonia region of Brazil, who as little as 10 years ago had their first contact with the modern world. Now, only six members of the tribe survive. They are all related and so cannot marry, and it is expected that the tribe will cease to exist within a generation.

As recently as May 2008, a previously unknown tribe was discovered in the Brazilian state of Acre. A light aircraft flew over their village twice in one day, taking photographs on the second pass. In the time between the flights, most of the women and children had

When tribal people encounter "civilization," the results are often harmful to their old way of life. Traditional skills are forgotten, disease kills many, and ultimately their independence can be lost.

A Peruvian Indian takes part in a rally in Lima. A growing number of confrontations are occurring between indigenous peoples and the police. Governments and tribes come into conflict as tribes see promises broken and lands stolen from them.

fled and the men had painted their bodies and were clearly ready for war. It was apparent that they realized that contact with the outside world meant danger.

In Brazil, tribes now have their rights to the land protected by law, but ranchers and loggers often get around this by wiping out all the Indians who were living there. It is clear that much better protection is needed for these people if they are to survive, let alone continue their traditional way of life.

Plundering the forests

Other countries do not give even the same levels of protection as that found in Brazil. In neighboring Peru, for example, up to 70 percent of the remaining forests are earmarked for exploitation by logging, mining, gas, and oil-exploration projects. Peru's president, Alan Garcia, has openly questioned whether tribes never contacted actually exist, though given the rate of forest destruction, this hardly matters.

Expert View

The plight of the natural world does not get any easier:

"What is happening in this region [of Peru] is a monumental crime against the natural world, the tribes, the fauna and is further testimony to the complete irrationality with which we, the 'civilized' ones, treat the world."

Jose Carlos dos Reis Meirelles Junior, FUNAI (the Brazilian government's Indian affairs department)

Creatures in crisis

It's not just people who are in danger as the forests come under pressure. The world's rain forests are home to at least 50 percent of all animal and plant species on the planet. This means that when large areas of rain forest are destroyed, sometimes whole species of animals or plants disappear with them. The particularly tragic thing is that sometimes we probably don't even know a species has become extinct, because nobody had discovered it before it was killed off.

Perhaps the most expressive of the great apes to human eyes and among our closest living relatives, orangutans are witnessing their habitats being destroyed at an alarming rate.

Orangutans in danger

In Borneo and Sumatra, in Indonesia, the rapidly growing palm oil industry is threatening the survival of one of our closest relatives from the animal kingdom—the orangutan. About 25 million acres (10 million hectares) of rain forest have so far been cleared to make way for palm oil plantations, which was responsible for at least half of the destruction of the orangutan's habitat that took place between 1992 and 2003.

FORUM

The needs of people and those of the native fauna and flora often come into conflict:

"The oil palms will bring prosperity to our country while providing cleaner fuel for the world. We don't wish to see orangutans wiped out, but they cannot stop our country's development."

Government minister, Borneo

"Cutting down the forest to grow oil palms will further restrict the orangutans' habitat. Can you allow that to happen?"

Conservationist

What's your opinion?

Sadly, almost 90 percent of the planet's orangutan habitat has been destroyed. There are now thought to be as few as 60,000 orangutans left in the wild, and of these up to 5,000 are being lost each year. This means that the orangutans could have as little as 12 years left before we destroy them all. Humans are not setting out to destroy the orangutan, but they want the orangutans' forest home for palm oil plantations. This is a tragic example of how human "needs" and those of rare species come into conflict.

More species in danger

Orangutans are not the only creatures facing a bleak future. There are probably only 400 Sumatran tigers left in the wild, again because of the destruction of their jungle home for palm oil plantations. Meanwhile, in the Brazilian Amazon, there are fewer than 1,000 golden lion tamarins (a kind of monkey) left. Wherever humans destroy rain forest, animals and plants become endangered.

Are we losing vital medicines?

We cannot be sure of how many plants with possible medicinal uses are being destroyed before they can be properly investigated, but we can be pretty sure that it is happening. Stored in the forests awaiting discovery may well be as yet unidentified cures for diseases such as cancer, AIDS, and Alzheimer's disease. As noted, the rosy periwinkle of Madagascar is already being used in the treatment of some types of cancer.

An extract from this colorful plant, the rosy periwinkle, is used to treat leukemia. It is impossible to know how many more potential cures remain undiscovered in the rain forest or how many more we have already destroyed.

Chapter 5

How do we address the problem?

Most, if not all, of the new ways that formerly forested land is used have a negative impact on the environment. With the burning of rain forest now one of the main human contributors to greenhouse gas emissions, people are beginning to see that something has to be done to stop the destruction.

Money for nothing

"Carbon offsetting" is a much promoted solution to the problem of climate change. It involves big polluters in the rich, industrialized countries paying countries in the developing world to preserve their rain forests rather than burn them.

The idea of receiving money for not burning their forests could encourage developing

Expert View

Michael Somare is the spokesman for the Rainforest Coalition of more than 30 rain-forested countries:

"If we, the rain-forested nations, reduce our greenhouse gas emissions, we should be compensated for these reductions."

Michael Somare, prime minister of Papua New Guinea

The main initiatives of the Rainforest Coalition, headed by Michael Somare, include reducing carbon emissions and sustainable forestry. The coalition sees carbon trading as a key factor in achieving its objectives.

This oil refinery is in the US. Is it right that industrialized countries should be allowed to pay developing countries to preserve their rain forests in return for the right to continue their polluting activities at home?

countries to threaten to burn theirs down in order to receive carbon-offset money. It also begs the question: who gets the money? It is unlikely that the people who actually live in the forest and make their living through low-level agriculture will see any of it.

Relocating the problem

On the face of it, "making the trees worth more alive than dead" seems like a good idea, but it has some major flaws. Carbon offsetting could be used by the most polluting industries in the West to enable them to continue their bad habits at home. If we allow these industries to pollute at the same rate as they are now while paying to keep forests standing in distant parts of the world, we will not stop adding to the greenhouse effect. We will, at best, see no change and, at worst, see a net increase.

Another issue is that by stopping deforestation in one area through the use of carbon offsetting, the problem might simply move to a new area of forest. This new area of forest might have even greater value due to the amount of carbon it stores or because of its greater biodiversity or the number of local livelihoods it supports.

Could it really work?

If carbon offsetting can be properly managed and industrialized countries pay offsets that are distributed among the people in rain-forested countries who really need to benefit from them, then it could work. For example, Peru plans to preserve 133 million acres (54 million hectares) of forest and is aiming for zero deforestation in 10 years. To achieve this, it says it will need to receive $25 million per year for the next 10 years.

Nature reserves

Some non-governmental organizations (NGOs) have forged successful partnerships with national governments to create nature reserves in the rain forests. One example is the Harapan Forest in Sumatra, Indonesia. Here groups of NGOs from Europe and Japan have joined forces to halt logging in a 250,000-acre (101,000-hectare) area of lowland rain forest that is home to 267 bird species, 66 of which are at risk of extinction, and endangered mammals such as the Sumatran tiger, Asian elephant, and clouded leopard.

Prince Charles visited the Harapan Forest in 2008 as part of a tour of Indonesia. An avid conservationist, the British prince is one of many prominent personalities who are lending their support to the preservation of the rain forest.

Harapan is the Indonesian word for "hope," and now there is certainly hope for the future of this forest, which was likely to be felled and replaced with timber or palm oil plantations. Although damaged, conservationists believe that it can be allowed to return to its natural state. The reserve will provide jobs for local people as wardens, forest guides, and plant nursery workers. In the long term, a research station and eco-tourist facilities are planned for the site.

The Harapan reserve is a great step forward for conservation and could show a way forward for other areas of rain forest. Obviously, the rare and endangered species found in the Harapan Forest have made it something to protect for the future.

Sustainable forestry

As a result of shoppers living in developed countries increasingly buying sustainable products, more of the forestry that takes place in rain forest areas is sustainable. This development is good for the inhabitants of forest areas since they do not have to overexploit their natural resources.

Many rare and endangered species, such as these beautiful clouded leopards, are found in the Harapan Forest reserve. Clouded leopards can run headfirst down tree trunks and hang upside down from branches by their hind feet!

For example, the Guatemalan community of Uaxactún (pronounced WASH-ak-toon) has received support from the Rainforest Alliance in its harvesting of xate (SHA-tay) palm leaves, which are often used in flower arrangements in the developed world. It's a big market, too—30 million xate fronds are delivered to the US and Canada each year for Palm Sunday celebrations.

Shipments of xate leaves from Uaxactún have so far earned the villagers $100,000 a year, with more than half of this going to the actual pickers. Normally, about half of the leaves exported are of poor quality and are thrown away. The pickers in Uaxactún have been trained to select only the best-quality leaves, which means that the palms can regenerate more quickly and the villagers earn extra for their work.

FOCUS

Investing in the future

"At the beginning, we felt inconvenienced—we said, 'we're poor, and they want us to make these investments.' But in the long run, we realized that those changes were essential for improving our forest management and addressing the basic needs of our community."

Benedín Garcia, founder member of the Conservation and Management Organization, Uaxactún, Guatemala

Sustainable forest agriculture

In some rain forest areas, attempts are now being made to make agriculture sustainable. This means growing crops in a way that is more in harmony with the environment, reducing impacts on the soil, and eliminating need to keep moving on every few years as the soil becomes depleted. Farmers who choose to farm sustainably can gain certification that allows them to charge higher prices for their crops.

Sustainable agriculture aims to cause less water pollution by controlling the use of pesticides and fertilizers, the chemicals in which either filter down through the soil to enter the water table or run off the land into drainage ditches and rivers. Soil erosion is reduced by planting on natural contours in the ground and by retaining a covering of trees to hold the soil together. Important wildlife habitats are protected, with buffer zones on riverbanks and wetlands and forest patches preserved.

The by-products of agriculture, including banana stems, coffee pulp, and orange peels, are used as natural fertilizer for the soil rather than just thrown away. Waste, such as glass, plastic, and metal, is recycled where possible. Water use is also observed and controlled to make sure that there is no waste. Farmers plan their activities better and take care to ensure that their farms improve over time.

Workers' benefits

Workers on certified farms have much better working conditions, with decent wages and housing and clean drinking water. They and their families have access to school, transportation, health care, and training. Sustainable farms tend to have more efficient

There is a growing market for sustainable and fairly traded coffee—a product grown in many rain-forested countries. Using new techniques, coffee can be produced in a way that minimizes damage to the rain forest.

Beatrice Sebyala checks the plantain crop on her organic farm in Uganda. Her farm is used as an example to others who want to learn the benefits of farming organically. Growing in harmony with nature is now seen as a viable and profitable option in many rain-forested countries.

workers, who give better productivity and produce better-quality crops than their less ecologically conscious rivals.

Everybody wins

Although it takes more time and effort to farm sustainably, the benefits are clear. Certification from an organization such as the Rainforest Alliance enables farmers to sell their crops for higher prices when they take them to market, and certification also makes it easier for them to access credit to invest in further improving their farms. The sustainable farmers also cooperate with conservationists to try to ensure that species and habitats are protected. Sustainable agriculture has so many positives that it seems to be an excellent model for the future.

Currently, an international organization, the International Agriculture Network, is active in 20 rain-forested countries in South and Central America, Africa, and Southeast Asia. It has almost 50,000 certified farms in its network, which in total cover an area of almost (1.4 million acres) 574,000 hectares.

FOCUS

Inspiring first step

"We hope it inspires many companies to make certification commitments—and that eventually all cocoa is from certified cocoa farms."

Matthias Berninger, Global Head of Public Policy, Mars, Inc., on that company's decision to buy Rainforest Alliance certified cocoa

The main obstacle to developing initiatives such as these seems to be training and persuading the farmers to adopt sustainable practices—and the money it costs to make the training and persuasion possible.

People matter, too

For any of the possible solutions to the problem of deforestation to work, the people who live in the forest have to be involved in every step—from coming up with ideas to implementing them. If they are left out of the process or driven off their land to make way for wealthy landowners or international companies, they will be more impoverished and forced to make a living by destroying new areas of forest.

The small-scale agriculture that forest people tend to practice involves crop rotation—the planting of different crops each year to give the soil time to recover. Their methods actually help the forest to grow and so do no lasting damage to it. Certification schemes and other schemes that provide farmers with a small amount of cash to help them establish themselves encourage entrepreneurship and provide greater incentives for them to manage their forests sustainably.

Many tribes have existed for centuries in the rain forest, living in harmony with their environment. Sustainable forestry and farming techniques may give them the opportunity to retain their traditions in the future while generating an income for trade with the industrialized world.

It is important that the forest peoples have their land rights recognized. They depend on the forest not just for food, but for shelter, medicine, and an income. If their lands are theirs by law, they have even stronger reasons for making sure that those lands are protected.

No quick fixes

If solutions for deforestation are to work, they need to take into account the drivers of destruction—the underlying problems that motivate the action—not just the immediate causes. Paying a cattle farmer not to cut down an area of forest one day will not stop him from going elsewhere and cutting down another patch of forest. The underlying problems need to be addressed—in this case, demand in the beef market and the competition for land that pushed the farmer to the edge of the forest in the first place—if long-term solutions are to be found.

We need to find ways of allowing the people who live in the forests to make use of them without needing to clear vast areas and produce crops or cattle on a large scale. The message should be about quality, not quantity, and we should be prepared to pay a premium for goods that have been sourced from farms in the forest where sustainability is seen as the priority.

It is no use just throwing money at the problem. Much of the funding given to rain-forested countries in the past has ended up in the pockets of politicians and their friends. We need somehow to ensure that help reaches the people who actually live in the forests since these are the people who have the power and the ability to protect the forests for the future.

Small, sustainable farms are proving themselves in many rain forest countries. By causing minimal damage to the forest, the farmers protect their environment while growing valuable crops that command much higher prices from buyers.

Chapter 6

How can we help?

It might seem that you can do little to help. The rain forests are far away and the problems are so massive that even if you did go there (which would involve taking a carbon-emitting flight across the world) and protected a little patch of rain forest, it would not help that much.

Fortunately, there are plenty of things you can do that will make a difference. You have power as a consumer—you and your family buy things all the time, such as food, fuel, paper, furniture, and all types of wooden products and objects.

Shop to support the rain forests

There are many products in the supermarkets these days that carry a certification mark. These products, which include coffee, tea, cocoa, and bananas, tend to cost a little more, but it's worth it to know that the little extra you are spending is helping to maintain a sustainable farm somewhere in the forest.

Look for the logos

The next time you are shopping, look for either a Fairtrade or Rainforest Alliance logo. These are issued by the Fairtrade Foundation and Rainforest Alliance, and both show that the farmers who grew the crop received a fair payment and that their workers had good working and living conditions. The logos are also a sign that the crop was grown on a farm where protection of

The most ethically produced and least environmentally damaging food products don't tend to be the cheapest. However, the small price premium helps to protect the rain forests and provide a better standard of living for the farmers.

Look for products with the Fairtrade logo. *Ubuntu* **is a South African word from the Bantu language meaning "I am what I am because of who we all are."**

the environment is taken seriously. In the case of the Fairtrade Foundation, it pays a guaranteed minimum price, which is currently much higher than the market price for a crop such as coffee. The Rainforest Alliance does not guarantee a price for its farmers, but most still earn considerably more than non-certified growers.

Where big companies work with the farmers to buy certified products, they give the farmers advice on how to improve their profits.

Avoid palm oil

Look at the list of ingredients printed on the packaging when you are shopping. If an item contains palm oil, try to avoid buying it. Rain forest will have been destroyed to make way for the palms. This is not easy, however, as palm oil is found in one in 10 supermarket products, including soap, chocolate, and even toothpaste.

Ethical wood

When buying products made from tropical wood, such as furniture and paper—some paper is still made from tree pulp from Indonesian—look for the FSC (Forest Stewardship Council) mark, which shows that the wood has come from forests where the rights of tribal people are respected and where the trees are cut in a managed and sustainable way.

Expert View

Expert advice and changes in the way we look at situations can provide answers to problems—such as the use of chemical fertilizers:

"The price paid for coffee is only half the solution. For instance, we have transformed the coffee pulp, which used to be discarded, into fertilizer. The farmers now don't have to spend money on fertilizer."

Mario Cerutti, head of coffee buying, Lavazza coffee

Adopt your own rain forest

Some organizations allow you to adopt an acre of rain forest in return for a donation. The money you pay is used to buy new land, to plant trees, and to pay staff to look after the forest and prevent poaching or other types of misuse. You don't actually get to own the forest you adopt, and not all the schemes are honestly operated, so make sure your money really is going to be put to good use by making donations to well-known and well-respected organizations or those that come recommended from a source you trust.

The Rainforest Alliance has some great rain forest adoption schemes that make a real difference—one example being the Bosque El Imposible National Park in El Salvador, which is made up of 9,000 acres (3,642 hectares) of rain forest. Since El Salvador has only 2 percent of its original rain forest left, the park is key to the survival of many species in the country. Rainforest Alliance works with local groups to protect the Bosque El Imposible from destruction by new coffee plantations or roads. Instead, it promotes shade-grown coffee to local farmers. This is coffee grown under tree cover, which means that birds in particular do not lose their homes and the rain forest suffers only minimal damage.

A farmer in Nicaragua prepares to package the coffee he has shade-grown on his small farm. The coffee he produces here supports him, his wife, and their four children.

Volunteer schemes

For young people (usually over 18), there are many conservation projects that allow volunteers to go to the rain forest. These provide the opportunity to experience life in the rain forest working alongside local communities. Through these volunteering projects, people can become involved in monitoring important species, improving facilities for people living in the forests, or promoting more sustainable farming and forestry.

Working vacation

Normally, volunteers are expected to pay for their experience—and the cost could be substantial, depending on where you go and how long you stay. But you do get an unforgettable trip to the rain forest, the experience of working in challenging surroundings, the opportunity to meet many other like-minded young people, and the knowledge that what you are doing is making a difference.

FOCUS

Journey of a lifetime

"Our journey took us . . . for an amazing trip down the Madre de Dios River. This journey was a fantastic opportunity to spot plenty of wildlife, including capybaras [the world's largest rodent], caiman [a type of crocodile], monkeys, and a great variety of birds. What a start!"

Alex Prior, conservation volunteer

This isn't for everyone, but for those wanting an adventure, perhaps during the summer between high school and college, this is worth thinking about.

In conclusion

There is no doubt that the rain forests are a magical treasure chest of species or that humans are destroying them at an alarming rate. Only now are we waking up to what we are doing. We must all pressure governments and big business to ensure that these precious forests are protected for the future.

The Amazon rain forest is home to amazing creatures, such as this capybara—the largest rodent on the planet. It can grow up to 4 feet, 3 inches (1.3 meters) in length and weigh up to 144 pounds (65 kilograms).

Glossary

biofuel A fuel produced from dry organic matter or combustible oils produced by plants.

buttress roots Roots that stand above the ground to provide trees with support.

canopy The top layer of trees, consisting of branches and leaves. The canopy acts like a roof over the tropical forest filtering out much of the sunlight before it reaches the lower layers of forest.

cash crop A crop grown for maximum profit rather than to feed the farmer and his or her family. Coffee, tea, bananas, palm oil, and soybeans are all examples of cash crops.

climate change A regional change in temperature and weather patterns.

conservation The preservation of the natural environment.

deforestation The clearing and destruction of the forest, often to allow farming or cattle grazing to take place.

desertification The gradual transformation of habitable land into desert, usually caused by climate change or by the destructive use of the land, including deforestation.

developed countries The wealthiest nations in the world, including those in Western Europe, the US, Canada, Japan, Australia, and New Zealand. Also referred to as industrialized countries.

developing countries Less economically developed countries, including India, China, and many Asian and African countries.

ecosystem A group of living things plus the non-living things they depend on.

endangered species A species whose numbers are so small that the species is at risk of extinction.

equatorial climate Relating to places that are situated near the equator and that are hot and wet throughout the year.

exploitation Taking advantage of something for one's own ends.

floor layer The layer resting on the forest floor, made up mostly of dead and decaying plant and animal matter.

fossil fuels Fuels, such as oil, coal and natural gas, that are formed from the fossilized remains of plants and animals.

global warming An increase in the temperature of the earth's atmosphere. Global warming has occurred in the distant past as a result of the earth's natural cycles. Today, however, the term is used to refer to planetary warming linked to human activity.

greenhouse gases Gases in the atmosphere that trap the sun's heat, resulting in global warming.

HEP Hydroelectric power, a means of producing power through the use of the gravitational force of falling or flowing water.

indigenous Originating in and characteristic of a particular region or country. Often used to describe the native peoples of various countries and regions.

intensive agriculture An agricultural production system that, relative to the land area being farmed, uses large and expensive machinery, large numbers of people, or is reliant on technologies such as expensive pesticides and chemical fertilizers.

liana A vine that grows up the trunks of trees.

nutrient cycle The uptake, use, release, and storage of nutrients by plants and their environments.

nutrients Substances that provide the essential nourishment for plants and animals to grow and live.

photosynthesis The process by which plants convert sunlight, water, and carbon dioxide into food, oxygen and water. The plants "breathe in" carbon dioxide and "breathe out" oxygen.

plantation A large estate or farm on which crops are raised, often by resident workers.

regeneration The natural growing back or bringing back into use of something, such as a forest.

shifting cultivation A system of agriculture where farmers move from one place to another when the land becomes exhausted.

shrub layer The layer of the rain forest that is above the floor but under the canopy.

subsistence farming A system of agriculture or livestock raising where virtually all the produce is consumed by the farming family.

sustainable project A type of development that meets the needs of the present generation without compromising the ability of future generations to meet their own needs.

Further information

Books

Butterfield, Moira. *Rainforests in Danger (Protecting Habitats)*. Franklin Watts, 2008.

Morgan, Sally. *Saving the Rainforest (Earthwatch)*. Franklin Watts, 2000.

Platt, Richard. *The Vanishing Rainforest*. Frances Lincoln, 2003.

Websites

www.foe.co.uk
  Friends of the Earth's website. Good information on rain forests, mostly hidden, so use the site search facility.

www.rainforest-alliance.org
  Great site with comprehensive information on the work of the Rainforest Alliance.

www.rainforestconcern.org
  Excellent site from this UK-based rain forest charity. Great information on their work and comprehensive resources for education.

www.rainforestfoundationuk.org/www.rainforestfoundation.org
  Websites for the Rainforest Foundation in the UK and US. Plenty of information on Sting's charity and its work in Central and South America and has good resources for young people.

www.rainforestsos.org
  Site for the Prince's Rainforests Project—news and information from Prince Charles's rain forest charity.

www.rethinkforests.com
  A site about managing healthy forests in the US.

www.savetherainforest.org
  Basic site with some good ideas and information.

www.ypte.org.uk
  The Young People's Trust for the Environment's website. A huge range of resources for young people, including a number of fact sheets on rain-forest-related topics.

Index

Entries in **bold** are for illustrations.